TIME
FOR KIDS
READERS

What's the Season?

by Alan M. Ruben

Harcourt
SCHOOL PUBLISHERS

Orlando   Austin   New York   San Diego   Toronto   London

Visit *The Learning Site!*
www.harcourtschool.com

In summer, it is hot. We go to the beach or pool.

In fall, it is cool. We rake the leaves that drop from the trees.

In winter, it is cold. We wear warm clothes and
play in the snow.

In spring, it is rainy. We use umbrellas to stay dry.

The sun shines in every season.

Rain or snow falls in every season.

What is the season now?